Reading & Writing

Modern Times

Reading & Writing

Modern Times

Marshall Cavendish
Benchmark
New York

This edition first published in 2009 in North America by Marshall Cavendish Benchmark.

Marshall Cavendish Benchmark
99 White Plains Road
Tarrytown, NY 10591
www.marshallcavendish.us

Copyright © 2003 Italian edition, Andrea Dué s.r.l., Florence, Italy

Library of Congress Cataloging-in-Publication Data

Silva, Patricia, 1963–
  Modern Times / by Patricia Silva.
    p. cm. — (Reading and writing)
    ISBN 978-0-7614-4322-3
    1. Books and reading—History—Juvenile literature. 2. Learning and scholarship—History—Juvenile literature. 3. Printing—History—Juvenile literature. 4. Writing—Materials and instruments—History—Juvenile literature. I. Title
    Z1003.S587 2009
    028.9—dc22
                                                2008032286

Text: Patricia Silva
Editing: Cristiana Leoni
Translation: Erika Pauli
Design and layout: Luigi Ieracitano
Illustrations: Alessandro Baldanzi, Lorenzo Cecchi, Sauro Giampaia, Luigi Ieracitano

Photographs: by courtesy of Federico Motta Editore pp. 22, 23;
Artothek pp. 6 (bottom), 8-9, 25 (bottom left);
Adam Woolfitt/Corbis p. 18; Catherina Karnow/Corbis: p. 19;
Farabolafoto pp. 16, 26; Scala Archives p. 15; Skoklosters Slott p. 6 (top)

Printed in Malaysia
1 3 5 6 4 2

Contents

Available to All

In the 17th and 18th centuries, intellectuals began to meet together in what were known as academies or *salons*. These salons were places for scholars to exchange ideas, theories, and the latest information on a great variety of topics. Many of these ideas would eventually be published in journals issued by the individual academies and available to the public. This free availability of knowledge contributed greatly to the spread of literacy and the desire of people to be able to read.

In the 18th century, the first great modern encyclopedia was printed, *L'Encyclopédie*, edited by the French intellectuals Diderot and d'Alembert. It was a colossal work that attempted to collect and present to the general public the most recent scientific advances in

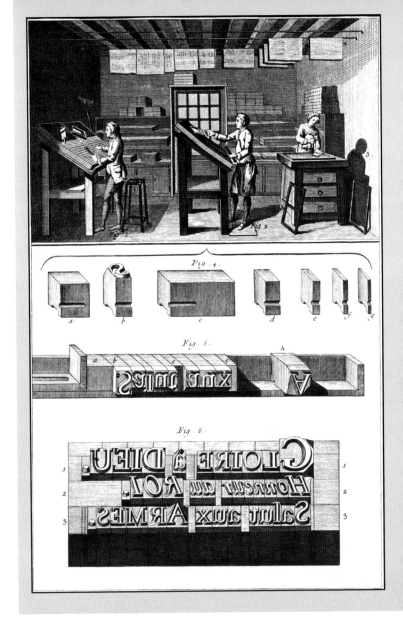

...ot: This plate
...1 Diderot and
...embert's
...*yclopédie* shows
...e composed for
...ting.

...osite, top: The
...n-century Italian
...t Arcimboldo
...ted fantastic por-
...s with faces made
...ruit, flowers, or ani-
...s. This painting of a
...arian is, appropri-
...y, composed of
...ks.

...posite, bottom:
...is scene depicts the
...ding of a newly
...eased book in a late-
...h-century Parisian
...on. The rich and the
...tured gathered to
...en and comment
...the texts that
...erested them.

all fields of study. This grand editorial enterprise directly influenced the rapid technological progress of the following century and helped give birth to modern industry.

Off to School

During the 19th century, many countries made education obligatory for all elementary school-aged children. As a result, the literacy rate—the number of people who could read and write—grew enormously

Opposite: School-children in the 19 century used hand held blackboards erasers for their les

and these people began to demand more and more material, such as books and maga-zines, that they could read and enjoy.

The 19th-century school was different in some ways from a typical school today. Schools often consisted of only one room where students from all different grades met together. Children used handheld blackboards and chalk to copy down their lessons and practice their handwriting. Once they had mas-tered writing their letters, students began writing their lessons using paper and nib pens dipped in inkwells.

Left: With students from so many different grade levels all in one room, teachers sometimes had to be strict to maintain order in the classroom.

New Ways of Writing

Each generation has had its own writing tools, from the stylus and brush of the ancient Egyptian scribes to the quill pen of monastic scribes. In the middle of the 1700s the first metal writing pens began to appear. These pens were generally made of steel, but occasionally even precious metals such as gold were used.

At the beginning of the 1800s, wooden pens fitted with metal nibs were popular. In the early 20th century, these instruments were used by students. The fountain pen also existed at this time, but it was considered a writing instrument for adults and was often given as a gift on a special occasion.

Then, in the 1930s, Laszlo Biro was watching a game of bocce when he had an idea: if a small ball was inserted into a tube filled with thick ink, a person could write on almost any type of paper without causing messy drips and stains. You probably have one or two of these ballpoint pens in your backpack.

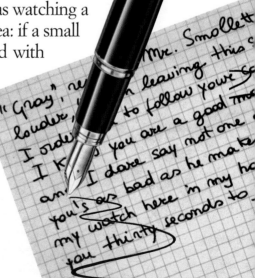

w: The metal-tipped nib pen
to be dipped periodically in
kwell to collect ink for writ-
As a result, drips and smears
: common.

39, 25
16, 14
10, 00
9, 80
7, 60
0, 55
1, 20
13, 00

$ 97, 54

Opposite: In 1883, the fountain pen was
invented. Its internal ink reservoir
eliminated the need for inkwells and
reduced the amount of drips associated with nib pens.

Right: A modern ballpoint pen

11

Striking the Keys

Before the typewriter came the writing cembalo. Its inventor had been inspired by the way a piano works: when someone struck a key, a hammer would move inside, hitting a cord and creating a sound. The way the first typewriters worked was also very simple. Small metal letters were attached to buttons or keys. The writer would strike the key and the metal letter would hit against an ink ribbon, and then make an impression of the letter onto a piece of paper.

The typewriter soon became a valuable addition to many offices because it allowed workers to quickly produce neat, legible documents. Today, however, most typewriters have been replaced by computers that, by the way, still use a keyboard similar to that of a typewriter.

v: In the early years type-
rs were used mainly by
workers. Many offices
had what were known
ping pools where many
ts worked together in
room.

Above: The first typewriters,
like the one shown here, were
very heavy and hard to move
around. Soon, however, a
lightweight, portable typewriter was developed. Some of
the first to use the new models
were reporters who took their
typewriters into the field and
wrote news reports where the
news was happening.

A Newfound Friend

In the middle of the 18th century, the Industrial Revolution transformed the print industry while simultaneously creating a new group of well-to-do readers who were eager to use their newly acquired literacy. Most countries made education obligatory, thereby broadening the circle of interested readers. Books became a new type of friend that spoke to the heart and mind of the reader.

Books caused their readers to dream, imagine, remember, laugh, and cry. They enabled readers to travel through time and space and helped them to explore the world and learn more about it.

Above: Gulliver's Travels, by Jonath Swift, was popula during the 18th ce tury. It was transla into many languag including Italian.

Right: The lower production cost for books created an increase in the number of bookstores. People began to purchase and keep low-cost novels, almanacs, and religious books in their homes.

People could take their favorite books to read outside on nice days. This woman has three books stacked on the bench.

The Illustrated Children's Book

Though today illustrations are often associated with children's books, the illustrated book has a long and prestigious tradition rooted in the great illuminated manuscripts of the Middle Ages.

In early printed books the illustrations were often printed in black outline and then hand colored. With the invention of modern printing techniques, book designers were able to print rich, multicolored images to enliven their texts.

Above: This illustration is an early children's book.

One of the most popular characters from an illustrated children's novel is Pinocchio. In *The Adventures of Pinocchio*, Carlo Collodi recounts the adventures and misadventures of the little wooden marionette who magically comes to life. Though first published in Italian in 1883, this story was reprinted all over the world in all the European languages as well as several Asian and African languages. Next to the Bible and the Koran, it became one of the most printed books in the world. In addition, the tale's popularity is such that at least 17 film versions of the story have been made.

PINOCCHIo

Opposite: An early Italian edition of Jules Verne's *Extraordinary Voyages* (*left*) and an illustration from Charles Dickens's novel *David Copperfield* (*right*).

Above: As books became more available, the interest in collecting them increased. Collectors and book lovers sought out special editions of their favorite works. These luxury books were generally printed on high-quality paper and handbound in leather. The covers were often lavishly embellished with gold lettering and designs called gold tooling.

Houses for Books

Libraries existed in ancient times. Egypt and Babylonia both had large libraries containing volumes written on papyrus or waxed tablets. The Egyptian library in Alexandria, in fact, is said to have held over 700,000 volumes on many topics arranged in a vast shelving system.

Royal and ecclesiastical libraries flourished in the Middle Ages, while personal libraries became popular during the Renaissance and into the 17th century. In the 18th century, the first private libraries were open to subscribers who paid a fee. The free public libraries we know today began to appear in the 20th century.

Opposite:
The Library of Congress in Washington, DC, houses one of the world's greatest collections of boo and manuscripts. The archives also includes maps, ph tographs, newspa pers, and music.

What Characters!

In the 15th century, when Johannes Gutenberg created his first series of movable type, he based the design of his letters on the formal handwriting of the time: the Gothic letter.

In the years that followed, many other printers designed alphabets or typefaces to use in printing their books. Many of these typefaces are still in use today and many are named for their designers, such as Bodoni named after the Italian printer and type designer Giovanni Bodoni. Other typefaces became known because of where they were used. The typeface Times New Roman takes its name from *The Times* newspaper for which it was designed.

Typefaces are usually categorized according to their different design characteristics, such as serif (letters with small bars at the ends, like Palatino) or sans serif (letters without bars, such as Helvetica).

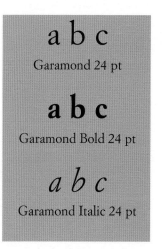

a b c
Garamond 24 pt

a b c
Garamond Bold 24 pt

a b c
Garamond Italic 24 pt

Left: Like most fo Garamond can be stylized in differen ways, including pl bold, and italic.

Opposite: Helvetic a sans serif font w Palatino and Time New Roman are serif fonts.

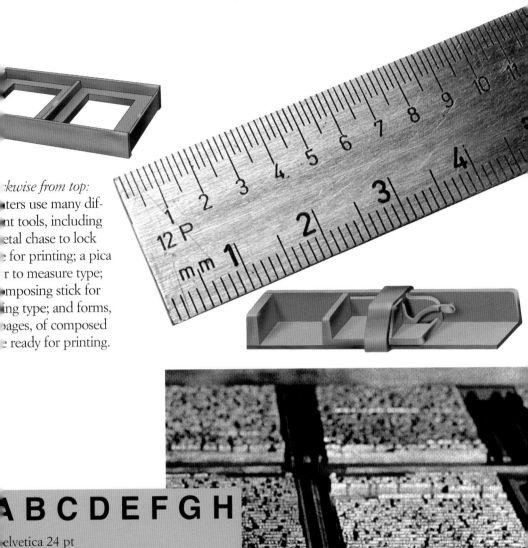

kwise from top:
ters use many dif-
nt tools, including
etal chase to lock
e for printing; a pica
r to measure type;
mposing stick for
ing type; and forms,
ages, of composed
e ready for printing.

A B C D E F G H

elvetica 24 pt

A B C D E F G H

alatino 24 pt

A B C D E F G H

imes New Roman 24 pt

Pressing Forward

In the 1400s Gutenberg used individual handmade metal letters assembled, or composed, by hand to print each page of his books. Later, in 1884, the Linotype machine was invented. It was a method of making metal letters using a machine that allowed the printer to create entire words or lines of type, thereby significantly speeding up the composing process in printing. In the 20th century, many printers began to adopt the new offset type of printing. Early offset printing used a photochemical method of etching letters and images onto metal plates. Once attached to a press, these metal plates would be mechanically inked and their images transferred to a piece of paper.

Below: A printer c poses type to creat page, called a form, is ready for printing

Above: A press for printing metal type.

Right: Workers compose metal type in a
[nineteen]th-century print shop.

[Off]set presses sped up the print-
[ing] process by mechanizing
[ma]ny of the steps.

Storehouses of Learning

In the 1800s, as the number of people who were able to read increased, the demand for leisure reading material grew. To meet this demand, publishers began to produce general interest magazines that appealed to a wide range of people.

Opposite: Early m
zines resembled c
logs, but it wasn't
long before they w
printed to appeal
all different intere

Magazines (from the French word *magasin*, meaning a general storehouse) were already in circulation in the 1700s. Some of the earliest magazines, which appeared in France, were catalogs of booksellers' inventory.

Essays and articles were eventually added to these catalogs, and soon periodicals were being published containing information on everything from women's fashion to fishing. These modern magazines became, as the French root word implies, true storehouses of reading and learning.

Hot Off the Presses

A daily newspaper is supposed to provide fast, timely information. A good newspaper collects, selects, and presents the news of the day, offering the most important elements of a story in an unbiased manner, thereby giving the reader the facts without passing judgment. The first true daily newspaper was the *Daily Courant* that came out in London in 1702. It was followed in 1704 by the tri-weekly *Review*, founded by the writer Daniel Defoe, famous for his novel *Robinson Crusoe*.

Right: Newspaper have helped inform their readers of m current events, such as this paper, announcing man's first landing on th moon on July 20, 1969.

Left and opposite: the beginning of th 19th century, young boys were hired to sell newspapers or street corners. The would shout out th headlines.

Special Forms of Writing

Writing can also take on special forms. In the 1800s a man named Samuel Morse invented an alphabet that people can hear! Morse used a key pad to tap out a message that was sent across telegraph land lines. His alphabet consisted of different combinations of short and long electrical signals. For example, the letter *A* was made up of one short tap and one long tap. Samuel Morse's invention came to be called Morse code.

Braille is another unique type of writing. The Braille alphabet was named after its inventor, Louis Braille, a Frenchman who had lost his sight at the age of three. In school, Braille became frustrated with the difficulties he faced in trying to learn to read and write. So, later in life, he dedicated himself to developing a simple system that visually impaired people could use to read and write.

Braille's system uses raised dots on a page to represent letters and numbers. The dots are placed in a series of cells. Each dot or combination of dots in a cell represents a letter or number. For example, a cell containing a single dot in position one is the letter *A*. A blind person can read these raised dots by lightly passing their fingers over the pages of text.

MORSE CODE ALPHABET			
A	.-	0	--
B	-...	1	.-
C	-.-.	2	..
D	-..	3	..
E	.	4	..
F	..-.	5	..
G	--.	6	-.
H	....	7	..
I	..	8	--
J	.---	9	--
K	-.-		
L	.-..	full-stop	.-
M	--		
N	-.	comma	--
O	---		
P	.--.	query	..-
Q	--.-		
R	.-.		
S	...		
T	-		
U	..-		
V	...-		
W	.--		
X	-..-		
Y	-.--		
Z	--..		

●●● ■■ ■■ ●●

S. O. S.

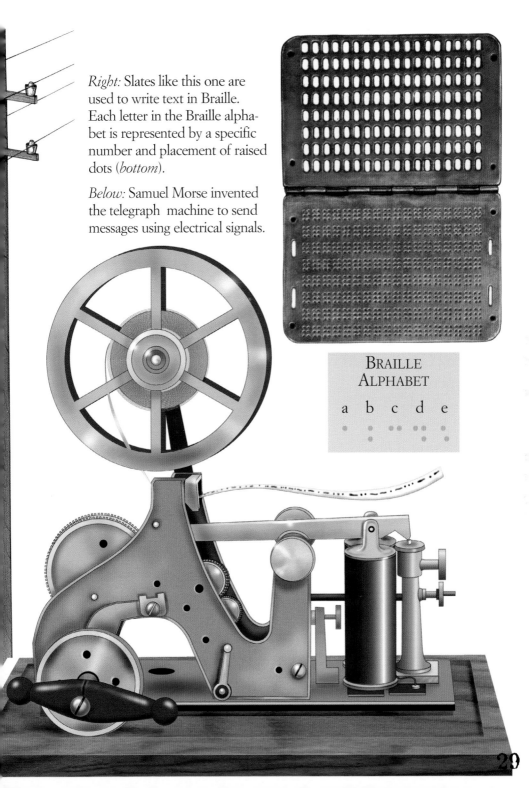

Right: Slates like this one are used to write text in Braille. Each letter in the Braille alphabet is represented by a specific number and placement of raised dots (*bottom*).

Below: Samuel Morse invented the telegraph machine to send messages using electrical signals.

BRAILLE
ALPHABET

a   b   c   d   e

29

Index

Page numbers in **boldface** are illustrations, tables, and charts.